CURES INCLUDE TRAVEL

CURES INCLUDE TRAVEL

poems

Susan Rich

White Pine Press / Buffalo, New York

WHITE PINE PRESS
P.O. Box 236
Buffalo, New York 14201
www.whitepine.org

With thanks to the following publications in which these poems first appeared:
Alaska Quarterly Review, American Poetry Journal, Bellevue Literary Review, Bellingham Review, Carapace (South Africa), *Clackamas Literary Review, Caffeine Destiny, Cimarron Review, Crab Orchard Review, Cranky, Elixir, Family Matters: Poems of Our Families, Folio, Green Hills Literary Lantern, International Poetry Review, O Taste and See: Food Poems, Natural Bridge, North American Review, Open Spaces, Poetry East, Poetry International, Prism International* (British Columbia), *Sea of Voices—Isle of Story, Seattle Review, Sojourner, The Sound Close In: Poems from the Third Skagit River Poetry Festival, Spillway, Water-Stone,* and *Witness.*

Cover painting: "An Early Exchange" by Mark Leithauser.

Publication of this book was made possible, in part, with public funds from
the New York State Council on the Arts, a State Agency.

First Edition.

10-digit ISBN: 1-893996-75-1
13-digit ISBN: 978-1-893996-75-5

Printed and bound in the United States of America.

Library of Congress Control Number: 2006923152

Special thanks to the founders, directors, and staff of the following residencies where many of these poems were written and re-written: Annamaghkerrig (Tyrone Guthrie Center), Centrum, Cottages at Hedgebrook, and the Helen Whiteley Center at the University of Washington.

Thanks also to Cindy and David Tracy of Katy's Inn, La Conner, Washington for their generous support and friendship.

Thanks to friends, faculty, and students at the Antioch MFA program in Los Angeles: Chris Abani, Sharman Apt Russell, Tara Ison, Eloise Klein Healey, and Brenda Miller.

Heartfelt thanks to Kelli Russell Agodon, Peter Aaron, Marcia Barton, Ruth Brinton, Mary Brown, T. Clear, Jeff Crandall, Victoria Ford, Neile Graham Linda Greenmun, Garrett Hongo, Kathryn Hunt, Kate Lynn Hibbard, Ilya Kaminsky, Kissley Leonor, Rosanne Olson, Ted McMahon, Linda Pastan, Peter Pereira, Carli Coetzee, Marge Manwaring, Ruth Brinton, Jennifer Markell, Janet Sekijima, and Gary Winans for reading and responding to these poems in various guises and disguises.

Thanks to friends and family who lent homes, ears, and cups of tea: Larry Blades, Debra Dean, Stephanie Delaney, Ian Keith, Jan North, Mary Pheelen, B. Ruby Rich, Hillary Salick, Eric Winiki, and Wendy Swyt.

Thanks to Dennis Maloney and Elaine LaMattina for their consistent support and belief in the work. You make it all possible.

Thanks to Jack Coulighan for the title and Mark Leithauser for the cover art.

Thanks to Artists Trust for an Artist Trust Fellowship, to the Jack Straw Writers Program, and Highline Community College for professional leave which allowed the time and space for many of these poems to come into being.

For Molly Daytz

Courageous Traveler

I. Guide Book

II Talking Geography

III Crossing Borders

At every step we take there are worlds upon worlds before us.

—*The Zohar*

We believe and disbelieve a hundred times an hour, which keeps believing nimble.

—Emily Dickinson

I.

GUIDE BOOK

Not a Prayer

Now with late afternoon light
rising off the floorboards and

gold-washed window frames,
a hushed air of attentiveness

massages walls to yellow streams.

The table in the vestibule,
oak chair, and lavender

blue bowl, show themselves to be
honey, butter, mustard seed.

And I take what is shimmering
into my body

stand still, living still, for the first time all day.

I wait for the sunlight to speak,
to remind me

how transformation happens
regularly as dusk enraptures day,

the half-averted gaze, the glass
of morphine placed by her bedside.

Flight Path

On the ascent I let go—
let my life drift
       to the side like litter.

In the complicity of wings
       I tend toward naming

freeway, river, mountain town—
       reaching beyond a horizon

where everything is travel, everything
       enlivened along its open path.

You ask if I'm lonely—

Is there a word for laundry
       dried in moonlight?

A name for the night cries
       of couples in early spring?

And if I could cajole the physical
       into sweet belief,

if a drop of honey on the tongue,
       could be *learning,* or say, *love.*

You ask why I go—

To where imagination holds
       the small blue craft of conversation,

to a life of evening song
    lived between the white spaces of now, of gone;

to come to pleasures of the heart, in the mouth,
    when the tongue conducts

    Star Thistle, Warbler, Petroglyph.

Listen, what if we could leave here—

with more than velocity, more
        than a thump, then a moan, could we

grasp the silver glint of sandpipers
        as they angle from water to air,

their bodies arced in unison
        hesitant, illumed, bare—

Change

He doesn't register me
as anything more or less
unique than the flawed light

the street lamp feeds to the hibiscus
tree that watches the corner
café of this empty street.

We collect here most evenings,
late, as if arranged, as if
we might share a scrap of

language and appear
legitimate as lovers:
for any passerby to see—

one body leaning
toward another, fingertips
meeting; *the figures blurred,*

an onlooker might say,
an odd pairing. How much
easier it is to acquiesce

to the alchemist's nation:
a new constitution, a policy,
findings of Truth and Reconciliation.

But this man right here
untethered from the ordinary,
still insists on his interior

gaze, his fraying chord
of grace. This man who nests
underneath the café eaves

tonight looks up and almost
nods to me—to me, not the stranger
from a distant country.

As he murmurs to himself
an indecipherable
blessing, I touch his

palms, pouring my change
into his two cupped
and gorgeous hands.

The Exile Reconsiders

Tonight, the tides pull through your shoulders
take up residence in between
your breasts, the teeth of the pocket comb.

Stars shoot themselves

along the edges of each year
and the night's purple darkness

finds you; refuses to go.

How to parse a palimpsest life?
The seasons

of paperwork traveling
like the magician's fist
disappearing one country for the next.

A legend of broken maps
in your bones

pale blue aerogramme by the phone.

Your grandmother's cattle,
rhythmic dots in the field,
leave a trail of milk on the tongue.

Tomorrow, the hoopoe inside you

will rise up
call above the seaboard—
cool mistress of turn and return;

mist-lit, two-fold, you'll leave
or linger here,
undiminished.

A Poem for Will, Baking

He stands before
the kitchen island, begins again
from scratch: chocolate, cinnamon, nutmeg;
he beats, he folds, keeps faith
in what happens
when you combine known quantities,
bake twelve minutes at a certain heat.
The other rabbis, the scholars,
teenagers idling by the beach,
they receive his offerings
in the early hours, share his grief.
It's enough now, they say.
Each day more baked goods to friends,
and friends of friends, even
the neighborhood cops. He can't stop,
holds on to the rhythmic opening
and closing of the oven,
the timer's expectant ring.
I was just baking, he says if
someone comes by. Again and again,
evenings winter into spring,
he creates the most fragile
of confections: madelines
and pinwheels, pomegranate crisps
and blue florentines;
each crumb to reincarnate
a woman—a savoring
of what the living once could bring.

Everyone in Bosnia Loves Begonias

On balconies safer than passport pages

bright, hard blossoms light up
bullet worn apartments. Amidst the cracks

from mortar shells—begonias—

Rex Begonias: the commonly
grown, taken for granted,

impossible to kill—
flowers are flourishing.

They work in the dirt.

While no one else in Europe
or America interferes,

like a strong neighbor,
the Rex Begonia is there—

in packs and tribes in Travnic,
Banja Luca, Prijedor,

guarding porch doors with serrated leaves—
preserving each family's story.

The Serbian soldier never imagined

the carbon dioxide source
that ricocheted his hand grenade

off the garden window. Across intermediary
boundary lines, strong-stemmed survivors

testify. The begonia has come a long way.
These partisans deflect all praise

for horticultural acts they've staged
and as it is with taxi drivers,

and cigarette vendors,
everyone in Bosnia adores begonias.

Bright light, no light—it's all the same to them:
budding begonias bursting

through the night.

Fissure

Around midnight, I'm driving
after losing my home, my now

ex-fiancé's words to me,
I can do better echoing

like the quick trill of car alarms,
fever pitched, three part, forlorn.

And while I'm waiting for the light
to change away from red,

away from my body
traveling alone,

the door locks down—

I notice the cramped shoulders,
the skin caked in white

grime and street dust, a boy's
body, legs outstretched,

sitting on a roundabout
in the middle of the night, in Cape Town.

Barefoot, broad faced, alone—
I've passed by him before, caught

in my lover's gaze, in jazz
riffs or the daily day old news.

And perhaps this blindness
can't be contained, but in this city

where children grow plentiful
as pomegranate seeds

on traffic islands, street corners, outside

the parking lot of every apartment
block—and this is harder

to admit, that our thirst rises
beyond response, beyond

what it seems any one of us could
reconcile, could believe:

the flint and fissure of our
time's brutality.

And this is why the child gives up
on begging for the night,

to take this roundabout
as his own; this unsheltered,

unremarkable, useless in a storm
cement circle with piecrust of stone—

because this is simply where the faltering world
can for one night remain contained;

here, where we all speak like beggars
with no precaution for the rain.

Photograph, May 10, 1933

Where one burns books, one will in the end burn people
—Heinrick Heine

At twenty-one, she is tired of learning
the subjunctive, assimilating the facts

inside her brain: cartography, the Ottomans,
the glory of Europe's trains.

So a torch light parade, bonfires by the opera house
sounded fine when her brother urged

Come on. She conjured human voices,
smoke filled cars, the pepper scent of men—

felt ready for conquest, to question the faith of angels;
ready for anything—anything but

an old manure cart dragged up
and down the library steps; Helen Keller

evicted along with Einstein, then Marx.
The orchestra collaborating

with the crowd, the familiar call
of classmates now locked in a medieval scene

and her brother joining in.
And so it begins on a pyre of light—

words spark, but the girl will avert her eyes
uncorked   inconceivable   pain.

A Poem for Mr. Raphael Siv
at the Irish Jewish Museum

Portobello, Dublin 8

Write a poem for the museum you demanded
as if you could order a poem the way you
order bread, toasted or with lox and cream cheese.

Or even one line. And this second plea
is what persuades me that you, Mr. Raphael Siv,
are a man who believes in poetry.

And why not? Aren't you Irish *and* Jewish?
a heritage any writer would covet,
hurriedly convert to, if it were that easy.

And clearly this vigil of yours lights its own
kind of artistry. When you set off to work each
morning, traveling down the South Circular

Road, can you sense the museum's
awakening beyond its curtains, prayer
shawls, and scrolls? As you open the interior

doors to the former Walworth Synagogue,
I imagine you welcomed in by the Shekinah,
your own bright avodah. Upstairs, the bride

will greet you; and the pews with their names
removed will recite a humble blessing
for their zaddik, their storyteller, for you.

The Sand Woman

A coat of granules stains her skin,
    her cuticles, eyelashes, hair;

        grains insert themselves
            into each meal of millet

    every peanut sauce she prepares.

        *

Stronger than brooms,
        it slips around Ottomans

    bed rolls, engulfs
    everything in the room.

        *

Sand flows between her toes

    swallows the threshold,
    and transforms small children

into convincing ghosts.

        *

On the Sahara's shore
        in the language of drift and dune,

of Harmattan and famine,
her life a prayer.

        *

The neighboring village
     turns overnight
          into a new nowhere.

      ✻

What can I do?
I rest then I get up again
I keep removing sand.

      ✻

And again she begins her morning
    an indigo scarf covering

and again, the accumulation
       sweeping the just swept room.

Mohamud at the Mosque

for my student upon his graduation

And some time later in the lingering
blaze of summer, in the first days
after September 11 you phoned—

If I don't tell anyone my name I'll
pass for an African American.
And suddenly, this seemed a sensible solution—

the best protection: to be a black man
born in America, more invisible than
Somali, Muslim, asylum seeker—

Others stayed away that first Friday
but your uncle insisted that you pray.
How fortunes change so swiftly

I hear you say. And as you parallel
park across from the Tukwila
mosque, a young woman cries out—

her fears unfurling beside your battered car—
Go back where you came from!
You stand, both of you, dazzling there

in the mid-day light, her pavement
facing off along your parking strip.
You tell me she is only trying

to protect her lawn, her trees,
her untended heart—already
alarmed by its directive.

And when the neighborhood
policeman appears, asks
you, asks her, asks all the others—

So what seems to be the problem?
He actually expects an answer,
as if any of us could name it—

as if perhaps your prayers
chanted as this cop stands guard
watching over your windshield

during the entire service
might hold back the world
we did not want to know.

For Sale

Xhosa women in clothes too light
for the weather have brought wild flowers
and sit sloped along the Claremont road.
I see her through rolled windows,

watch her watch me to decide if I'll pay.
It's South Africa, after all, after apartheid;
but we're still idling here, my car to her curb,
my automatic locks to her inadequate wage.

The dead eat blueberry scones for breakfast

with a touch of butter and sweet cream,
a cup of black coffee to reenact the morning;

some food, some drink, soon opens
awakening to a new place. One swan

keening as he circles our silvered lake.

The dead skim the headlines of the *Irish Times*,
re-imagine the aroma of eggs on toast;

they mime the domesticity we simply
breathe in and then just as recklessly let go—

our every action alive with their echo.

They're hovering at our shoulder
as we buy blood oranges

off the back of the young man's truck;
waving good-bye as he leaves

so suddenly. This evening the dead keep singing,

She is the belle of Belfast City,
then finger the jug of red wine

lingering near a woman's arms
alive in this careless air.

Mapping the Territory at Alki Beach

—for Richard Hugo

This year it's silver scooters that swirl
along the waterfront, weave between

walkers and runners, who field an unfurling
thread of golden retrievers—as if this

curve of world's washed clean, tucked-in
along its inland shore; bicycles

and pedal carts regularly swerve,
but somehow miss the sexy sunbathers,

miss the geriatric appraisers buying summer
sherbet drinks. Locals greet each other

Lovely evening, as one old woman travels
her archipelago of benches, one rest stop

to the next like a dog marks each blue hydrant.
She leaves her scent of honeysuckle,

leaves particles of sloughed off skin and a pear
so that next year a boy will run from his father's arms

using all his useless strength and shimmy-up
a splendid ruin; a sun-drenched, bird-marked,

fruit-stained bench, to shout from one
parallel point in time, *This globe is mine.*

Missing Home

Three days. Enough for everything
to catch fire, a gas leak, a sinkhole,

a bathroom pipe to expire.

Whenever I step away
from my swath of sky, my water lush

lip of the planet, I wonder

will the house survive
beyond the utterance of earthquakes—

And what about the cats?

Is Sarajevo shredding kitchen screens?
Otis stalking brown paper bags?

When did I convert to domesticity with a house key?

Is the clematis blooming?

The postman clearing his throat
with a clicking noise as he laughs?

Mr. Saturday Night

—for my student, Khalid

This could be an American story: drugs, discos, even
the Somali nickname that clings to you like an out-of-date

aphrodisiac. Living by chance in a Kenyan city, a mother's
rules flung across the lost luggage of border crossings,

her final dollars follow you: sixteen, exiled, on the edge
of sanity. You slip through an open window

riddled by a breath of mixed fortune. Money lighting
on hands with a warlord's stratagem until no one remains

rich enough to refuse you. Yes, American history.
Your daily regime of *qaat* dreams, as good a win as any.

Who will tell of the deep pleasure in tragedy? This
no waiting for tomorrow to bathe in the forbidden.

Yes—our red, white, and blue story. Now worlds
away, sponging up new nouns in a new country—

it's undercut by the stench of an abandoned body
you try not to step on in the creosoled street.

Early Impression

I adore living in a place where the mountain comes and goes.
Did you see the mountain? the people ask each other warmly
in the normal course of days—*there*—hovering over the Sound,

above the freeway, like a heavenly aunt above downtown.
We mean *our mountain* though Seattlites are savvy enough not to say—
snowcapped on summer evenings, omnipresent, slightly pink.

Nisqually 6.8

We stood on the earth like body surfers
given up to the motion of backward, forward,

our arms reaching out, uncertain if movement
emerged from interior or exterior weather.

Windows undulated outside whitewashed frames
while the world, in abeyance, sang—

Metal banisters attempted odd sounding sonatas
the trees at right angles ratcheted further and further

our hands reached out, holding on to each other
as strangers shared questions of depth and scale,

passing rumors of the miracle quake
that had left humans unscathed.

Although now I mistrust solid things:
rock, ferry dock, historical building—

I awake at night and the bed is still shaking.
Each crack in the sidewalk, the viaduct,

the excessive beating of one's own heart,
holds the afterimage; the Nisqually mark.

II.

TALKING GEOGRAPHY

"The past is never dead. It's not even past."
—William Faulkner

What You Americans Should Know: Partial Stories

We haven't been stateless all our lives
prepared with a satchel packed, a suitcase

grabbed in the middle of a life, but no map.
Just a number, meticulous on blue paper.

Maybe an old family friend, a half-brother's
half-sister, the aunt of Habiba's first husband

will arrange for the passports, the papers which
ferry us as far as Kismayo, revise birth

dates, clans, a lover's last words
so that by fall we're all unrecognizable.

Who are you, yaa tahay, who are you
in San Diego, Seattle, Toronto?

Bring frankincense, myrrh, maybe a high
school diploma, baby shoes hidden

in future view of all we are sure to lose.
What stays the same but the skin

we're traveling in and even then the cold air
burns inside our nostrils for weeks.

They say no one gets here from a straight
line, they say we, we are the lucky ones.

The Music of Things

If she were to listen in just the right way
to the corkscrew

what delicate knowledge
would ensue?

Could she redeem

the silvery gleam of the ice
cream scoop

with a sprig of lavender?

Cajole her mother's cookie-cutter half-moons
into clicking out old jazz tunes?

How would it change
the afternoon

if she spoke the language of the pastry flute —

a hieroglyphic text
someone once knew.

If she could hide away

among the Russian songs
of the salad tongs

translate the wayward notes

of her kitchen tiles
into an overture for an unborn child

keep the music playing for a little while.

Polishing Stars

My mother believed in the strength of labor
over love, she'd torture each microbe, disappear dust
on two bent knees bearing down on a faux marble floor.

And when it was scrubbed beyond question,
past reason, she'd call *Su-san*, handing me a faded rag
and ancient tin of something cool as resin:

A blue-green glaze to brush across the burnished rays
of copper shooting out beneath the breakfast bar;

at four, I played a worker cursing the ravaged stars.

The Women of Kismayo

The breasts of Kismayo assembled
along the mid-day market street.

No airbrushed mangoes, no
black lace, no underwire chemise.

No half-cupped pleasures,
no come-hither nods, no Italian

centerfolds. Simply the women
of the town telling their men

to take action, to do something
equally bold. And the husbands

on their way home, expecting
sweet yams and meat,

moaned and covered their eyes,
screamed like spoiled children

dredged abruptly from sleep—
incredulous that their women

could unbutton such beauty
for other clans, who

(in between splayed
hands) watched quite willingly.

*Give us your guns, here is our
cutlery, we are the men!*

the women sang to them
an articulation without shame.

And now in the late night hour
when men want nothing but rest,

they fold their broken bodies, still
watched by their wives cool breasts

round, full, commanding as colonels—
two taut nipples targeting each man.

White Lilacs One Year Later

That weekend we sat around the table belly-laughing
the way families were supposed to.
We knew it would be Mom's last birthday but didn't say
just worked harder to return home
our actions shaped in the extravagance of doom.

Is it still a birth-day when the birth has met its death?

The doctor shows me with his index finger, *Here,
there, can you see?* Seven crescents unnaturally bright
like moons I trace on the windowpanes at night.
The best, he says, *twelve weeks.*

In the evening I get out *The Book of Yiddish Jokes and Proverbs*
try out transliteration, *álefs* and *érevs,* until we are laughing
beyond language, my guttural *Loz zikh nit shpayen in der kashe*
transporting us until tears clot the soft powder on her face.

She doesn't push the chair back, put away the food
that will go bad, stack the dishes, pour the tea.
A good day, is all she says, undulating past me,
focused on the rise of carpet, the fluidity of feet.

Why isn't there a word for what today is?

In her bedroom we try out another kind of conversation:
Here, now, before speech fades again or escalates
to something else. She helps me slip off the shoes,
roll support hose from still shapely legs;
undo the girded hooks of her bra.

Is there a greeting to exonerate, white lilacs to console?

What happens next is what she hates the most—
the seconds it takes each night to slip the wig off;
her bald head gleaming, insistent as glowworms in the dark.
She places her palms on the sparse tufts as I keep watch.
Helpless in what my hands cannot touch.

Morning Mediation at the Alki Beach Café

I have dutifully played the girlfriend,
illicit lover, thief,
starred as the afterthought, the erotic dream—
I am the woman in the window
watching dog walkers and pearly-eyed mothers

who hip-hop along the promenade
with newly-fashioned prams racing
the infant into the world;
rushing round the point from lighthouse
to chowder house, the new portraiture—
mother and child running

where? Somewhere I could never go—
so quiet, so curly-haired.
And if I mark the box for *none of the above*

write in *a separate calling*
into silence, an attitude of heart
to travel many days alone;
and if I speak to no one

but the waitress: *coffee,*
scrambled eggs, sweet butter on the side,
eggs the French would call *confused;*

as the young girl in sexy top concludes,
I would rather suck my big toe
than stay with you and your need to be alone;
then how to play her tattooed lover,

without argument, just thinking, let's imagine,
of moist shins, full lips, sucking?
And here I must stake some claim—
I am a woman marking the middle distance.

I do not want to hire someone
to wash between my toes, to measure medicine
into a tube, to call me *honey-darling,*
prop the pillows. I abhor the wrinkles
appearing at my wrists, my hips

stretched along another triangle pose.
A man, dark hair, clear eyes, ambles by
my beach café, when he sees me does he mean to look

away or am I a slip of sunlight on the glass?
I could reach him at the water's edge
offer beach glass, limpet cups, martinis

at my place straightaway. Though now
he's tracking one of the running women,
pressing his clicker off and on—a squeak
and flash of lights from his new Humvee.

And what will he recall—
this moment of mid-morning, late April,
our lives glancing toward each other
and away in an instant wrangling
for *more, more, more*

which might reform the everyday
to a breath of air, each instant, a radiant indifference.

Annamaghkerig 4 A.M.

County Monaghan, Ireland

The later the hour, the more convinced
I become of voices outside
                traveling
through the courtyard, the conservatory;

opulent bass tones of men
        with a woman's brighter chatter.

        Up along the tree canopy
the phrases linger

        reassembling into light

        branches of laughter.

Sounds rustling each to each:
        Russian cheers, a Siberian drum beat.

(They must be soaked to the bone by now.)

In the teakettle's mist one small shout
        the timbre closer
                then further away

across to the other side of the lake.

Before morning comes,
        before I bow to the blue
shore and brave the sun

I listen again to the torn cloth of music.

Ghazal for Everyone

A war is like an epidemic, it happens to everybody.
—Andrea Barrett

Sides of beef in blue carrier bags strewn along the interstate's netherworld;
today marks day five of the war that invades my world.

A message from God? Overturned truck? Foreign objects?
Liberation instead of *invasion* makes a mockery of this world.

Restaurateurs erase *French fries, French roast, French toast,*
Champagne and Merlot disappear as if this will transform the world.

At the Statue of Liberty on Alki Beach, neighbors light their candles,
We will vote again someday in the not so distant world.

A woman appears with a cardamom cake, round and whole—the scent
of vanilla traveling from her kitchen into our rich and grieving world.

In Transit

French television has done a documentary on him. He shaves every morning, washes up
in the passenger lavatories and takes his clothes to the dry cleaners. The stewardesses give him food.

He will not beg and rarely gives himself
to speech, his attitude is what

you'd call removed.
And you would never know it

by his shoes or ivory suit,
the lightly chiseled cheekbones

hewn as if from translucent soap—
that he lives a life enclosed in the human

flow of check-ins, skywalks, carousels.
With his silver luggage cart,

his pipe, his books, his Mediterranean look—
Not homeless he assures you

just stranded—as if answering
the one resounding question, *Someone like you?*

Stranded, as if he has cast ashore
on an unfamiliar island

he claimed as Charles de Gaulle,
where under fluorescence, eleven years,

no holidays, no jasmine, no sex,
he's been carefully unraveling

the undertow of world affairs:
Tianamen Square, Rwanda,

the Middle East's fight against peace.
The airport is not bad he tells the TV

as he underscores his hard-won words
in seventeen journals of aquamarine;

scribbling until the terminal itself
becomes unmasked, unmoored, unglued—

until the flight attendants begin unfastening
their wings. *Please, have a seat,* he tells you, so you do.

Bosnia, Again

In a town near Sarajevo
renamed, redistricted, rebound,

I walk the avenue of parallel views:
the invisible boundary line

where money moves from marks
to dinars—license plates

from faded blue
to soft gray design.

Each post office hangs
a flag as if for a certain team.

And while the Muslims control water
and Croats electricity,

no one here breathes, and I imagine,
behind balconies of begonias,

no one sleeps.
Even after the war—

after accords and declarations,
the city refuses its name.

　　　　Late afternoon and children
follow me to the boardwalk

Give me your cigarettes,
give me your money.

More and more children come
until their small hands, their palms

and fingers are stinging
my breasts, prodding between

my legs, tracking me
through parks to just outside

a shop where a woman
observes the scene, takes me in

reluctantly, *This shop closes at five.*
Her eyes down as she sweeps.

Cleaning—and for good reason
this is what is disturbing.

       Outside again, boys and girls
swarm over me like bees. They dive

bomb silently.
The town is full of empty streets.

The Traveler's Tale

We played through to the dawn, pausing only for the cups of tea
he strained, poured and used to touch my hands—*Where have you*

come from, where are you going, he asks as if he will die if he
can't know—the move light as his upper forearm brushes my own.

Our figures recognizable across any pub—in the rhythms and cues
tracked by one unemployed window washer and me—

waitressing tables, a year, more, towards the Pyrenees: Is this all
attraction is made of? A Cadbury, a shandy? Perfumed rooms?

And then again questions—From? To? Soon there would be blood
pudding, bangers and mash. Much later, he'd be Mozart or Jesus,

inspired by a cracked violin, bible verse readings, an endless night
stream of talking to himself, to me, his three-year-old niece

in the border country. *Where have you come from? Where are you going?*
Whoever lost later there was this: a joy untold,
                                    a wound in moving pieces.

What the Baker Wants

To create sweetness, to make of nourishment an art,
as if the Book of Pastry could teach
each measured fold and sift of love—

Rum babas, rugelach, Charlotte royals.

He'll bring her burnt cream
for the earlobes, wild
raspberries slipped inside their simple clothes.

Peach ginger scones and a pecan loaf.

They'll press fingers
into sugar, flour, brandied butter,
well water bracingly cold;

their upper bodies lithe
as they sample the twist of a palmier,
cross the surface of a latticed fruit pie.

His daydream rolls onward like a chocolate roulade—

imagining late night debates.
What does the truth taste like? Thick as purple honey
or light as vanilla soufflé?

She'll offer him floating islands
praise the shape of his Paris-Brest,
his Gateau St. Honoré. And in the morning—

Warm brioche and almond toast.

Oh, what does the tongue know
that our hearts cannot?
Tiramisu and lemon tarts.

If You Could Lick My Heart

If you could lick my heart, it would poison you,
If you could click your long white coated tongue
Along the contours of what we didn't pursue,

Nullify the body with oleander, nightshade, yew;
What would you do with so much leading toward none?
If you could lick my heart, it would poison you.

Come, count the ways I've curtained the pain from view.
One, with an art for surviving, two, with a morning run
Pounding the contours of what we didn't pursue.

Rest assured, there's nothing you can do—
Not tears, nor sex, nor donations in large sums—,
If you could lick my heart, it would poison you.

It's finished now, this field guide of purple and blue
Which recorded each proof, a fable barely begun—
Held along the contours of what we didn't pursue.

The truth be damned—you were too weak to choose,
Between a luminous life, and the other, safer one.
If you could lick my heart it would poison you
Along the contours of what we might still pursue.

Special Reports

South Africa, 1997

She sprinkles snuff along the top of his tomb
tells him what is about to take place.

They've come for forgiveness
after all that they've done: the young men

burned to ash at braais, the Priest's
two hands bathed in the white light

of a letter bomb, a girl choking
chickens as she hides in the coop

desperate to stay alive. They've come
with no money, no proposal, no plan.

Each man cleansed and pink.
They've come for forgiveness.

She gazes away from the tomb
back toward the township, the streets

dense with children, the mothers' unease—
extras lined-up in a Hollywood movie.

With a lopsided stride, she finds her way
to the visitors, steps up proudly, fires

her mouthful of saliva, spitting dead
straight in the eyes of *forgiveness;*

one widow fine-boned and lean,
bows to the cameraman of the SABC.

Day 7: In the Beginning

Real horror remains uncircumscribable.
—NPR April 2003

Now the first story of Iraqi civilians
page seven of this morning's news:

194, 199, 278 *the reality is none of these figures...*

Last night an anchor
for Aljazeera apologized for explicit footage

of one twelve-year-old boy
his face frozen in a tranquil expression ——-

he could almost be asleep

except for the fact that half
his head had been blown off from the back.

The world should know the truth
the Aljazeera anchor said.

What is poetry in wartime?

After you've gone, the house

falls deep into disarray; dishes
cleansed by the cat's rough tongue—

his whiskers skate along the dinner plate's
gray rim; soon pyramids of underwear

rise above the hallway's long horizon.
Days I stay indoors answering to no one.

Seasons change, change back, unfinished—
rooms, half-painted, hold no door frames.

Light bulbs die, the wood stove's lacking fire;
some days you call, the voices overlap

trapped along a wire: *hello / good-bye/ hell hole.*
The lettuce leaves and worm bin mock desire.

Self-Portrait with Trampoline

Where wouldn't she go if she trampolined
into night,

above open fields
and orchards

of apricot, red plum?

What might she know if she basked
in her bright body,

in the seduction of flip
and spin,

the air tender as muslin?

Above the clock tower
and punk-lit roadside diner

she'd ascend
to where the glory of

a dozen blue martinis couldn't reach—

where the worry lines
of waitresses unfold

into a chorus of customer *oh's.*

Her limbs, hummingbird-light,
as undocumented dishwashers

rinse away grapefruit rinds
and remnants of peach pie,

faces to the window, a recognition in their eyes.

Then she'd feel the pulsing
of her own heart's gate

sense the rhythmical thump
of yes, of go—

somersaulting into the simplicity

of all she knows now
all she had always known.

Iska's Story

I.

From here the world seems random
        waves re-surfacing
                and waving again:

tank-bellied clouds, ducks' beaks, a guiltless sky.

II.

Days beget days
        and I try to shape an alphabet
                alarm across one simple page.

Iska says, *You can never really write what happened anyway.*
       It's like a hole that fills constantly with water.

III.

No rooting system on this sun-drenched beach,
no cosmic tide re-ordering;

nothing bright in what I have to say.

IV.

If war is a kind
        of handmade quilt,

her needles pierce torn portions of our lives.

V.

Iska repeats the story
unembellished, no flowers.
No forgetting in our four-hour interview.

VI.

Across from my cabin, the worn

weathered box
         of an old man's mobile home;

he's planted rows of plaid armchairs.

VII.

One guy was just going, throwing grenades
constantly at that hour. So whenever
anybody had to do chores

they had to do them before 5:00 P.M.
and then just go inside the house and pray to God.
Wait and see when you were going to be hit.

VIII.

Why not write another kind
of Somali story?

Iska slipping into Hollywood movies,
the pre-war cafés, French schools, fabric mills?

Late afternoons wandering
an angel-ringed promenade by the beach.

Children come home, eat dinner,
as a worried mother licks her son's elbow

her taste-test to see if the boy
had been diving in the sea.

IX.

This person got cut off both his legs.
This person lost an arm. This person lost a daughter.
This lady, she was cut into little, little pieces and

they couldn't find her body, so they
put the pieces together and the pieces came to
to   just   this   much.

X.

So perhaps wounds and words
don't work together.

Why try and reclaim unimaginable pain?

Everything happens for a reason,

Iska repeats. It's her ballast, her well-worn refrain.

> *And when it's your time.*
> *It's your time.*

XI.

Can you imagine?
          One religion, one culture.

We talk the same language
          but we cannot understand each other.

God took the blessing out of the language.

XII.

One minute you're chopping sweet potatoes
for dinner, a late sun-lit afternoon.

The next, the world explodes
and the porch upon which you're laughing

no longer exists.
A dozen cousins disappear in a crush

of chemical air leaving you blinded
and alone, or not alone.

          You are climbing up a wall.

XIII.

Someone in white lifts you up
alters your direction

          so that now
          you climb out of the rubble

out into the street. You are
blood-covered, shrapnel wedged in

like stickpins in your shoulder
but you're fine
and then there's no one there to thank.

No one wearing white
no angels here.

XIV.

Another frayed end and I'm back again
by a cabin in Fort Warden,

former home to military washerwomen.
And now

the fort complex becomes fodder
for artists, one dance

director oozes over the old abandoned bunkers.

Iska watches
as the director commands her company out at midnight

to dance barefoot on cement stages.
No, no angels here.

Fort Warden, Port Townsend, WA 2004- 2005

II.

BORDER CROSSINGS

"The opposite of a profound truth
may be another profound truth."
—Neils Bohr

What She Leaves Unspoken

When she is blue she is not kingfisher,
jacaranda, yew.

She is not a river tide

or drum roll; not a periwinkle
bolt of fabric,

a French matchstick
gone unused, but the grime on

beveled glass, the battered cup, the small

hole in your left shoe. She cannot move
one dormant arm above

the hydrangea of her mind—

no kitchen clock, no metronome measures
this conscripted time, this Tuareg scarf of blue.

She is a knot, a ridge, an open wound,

a clue without an answer. No country
tune, no catalogue of saints

can bring her out, across the way.

No, she is not air, nor unstitched wrist,
nor Mary's Bosnian brood;

when she is blue, she is not you
but an absent text, an unreliable X.

What saved me was geography,

not my mother, each morning scraping
the carbon from her burnt toast;

not the navy blue skirts shapeless
as New Mexico she'd sew each fall

and I, colonized once more,
would wash, then wear. Not

disappearing my plate of string beans
leaving no safe havens

no change in the earth's atmosphere.

Every night, the house set to sixty degrees
bedroom curtains unfolding

into a meridian of lava peaks
my father would listen, lean

his back against the tributaries
traveling over the blue closet door.

He'd offer up news of continental drift
the sidereal map of his days.

Look, he said, *there are faultlines in Zimbabwe.*

I knew he wanted to warn me
we would never give each other enough.

I'd stare at my desk, stumble over equations.
Give nothing away.

I'd wait for him to go, defeated,
lost in the unforgiving ridge of the Pyrenees

as I turned back to the atlas
the pages encoded with the will to leave.

In Search of Alternate Endings

Endings come subtle as shadows that interlace, then dissolve
on an ice-covered pond. The first I remember a hand on my breast—

at the small of my back, the uncovering of a secret life.
The knowledge that pain is always increasing.

Is there a form for how to tell this right? *Fat Man* and *Little Boy* explode
in the sky, concoct obscenity out of speed and light. I picture skeletons

of department stores—Bonwit Teller, Best & Company, New York's
Peck and Peck. Then the chrome curve of soda fountains, vinyl red 45s,

milk bottles chiming as they're abandoned by a patio step. Babies die
without being born, a helicopter lifts off, arms waving out of view;

and on an abandoned grocery cart, surrounded by chipped glass
and rags, is an intact, nearly frozen, banana chiffon pie. The occasion

of its creation so far from where we've just arrived. Hearts crack open,
an infant lost, but an appetite remains for kites and stars. In Japan,

a woman visits statuettes to her *mizuko jizo*, dresses the aborted fetuses
in crocheted robes; offers them handkerchiefs, faux pearls and dog figurines.

But where do I go to visit the ones who have died? Where do I bring
cocktail swizzlers and cuff links? Pop-up toasters, percolators,

a yellow lawn mower inked with the sweat of a lover? My could
have been taken by a man in white cloth who inserts Malaysian

pick-up-sticks inside a woman, oneself at twenty-five? The term gone
beyond weeks to months, three, four ... It's a universe with endings bright

as grief. To shower may mean the end of a life, gas spreading or
clear water next time. *Chelmno, Treblinka, Auschwitz.*

The Doctor injects a gypsy's veins with sea water, sews twins back to
back, cuts the breast from a woman, pats her head.

But this month preoccupied with the snow—
half-formed flakes on black birch accumulating like the ruffles

on a rich man's tuxedo. Is there grace in how to tell this light?
The exuberance of old pinball machines, dining cars, the body on a table,

anesthesia not doing its job. I miss easy injustice: a Paris Metro,
protection money, international law. *Hold my hand, hold my hand,*

is the mantra she sings as the vagina expands, the man works along,
pulling out pieces of skin, finger bones, an open jaw. And I'm asking

as one conglomerate of failed needs, I'm asking at the end
of sharp pain: what insists on this excessive, patterned dance?

My Mother Returns at Low Tide

Not her worn orange cardigan,
tissues bobbing from the sleeves
like a pair of playful trolls,

not her rump steak or soggy peas,
but I am becoming my mother
in a body I awake to each morning

which is not my body, my breasts
buried inside her breasts,
her falling spheres of fish-eyed pears.

And when I let the self hope,
try to fit within another miracle
fabric swimsuit, my words embrace

her golden, double-note of fate:
What a figure I've lost, where did it go?
What I can say for certain on this

floating bridge facing an impalpable
life at forty-six, on this bright sea-
salted morning, is that I seem no longer

myself, no longer Susan, no longer
a soft turquoise dress waiting
to answer to the weight of her own limbs;

but instead breathe in the mother
I never recognized, never learnt to hold
her sorrow like a stubborn starfish—

and then breathe out what I couldn't know:
to love a fish that is not a fish,
a star that will never reach the sky.

To My Mother, Dead Eight Years

When I travel out of country
you can't follow as easily; can't click
your tongue around my thighs'
circumference, chart my unsocial
social life. I've flown Cape Town to
Jerusalem fleeing condemnation
yet our cold words cling like the dying
roots of pot-bound plants: cracked, unforgiven.

But that's just half the days, half
the lines inside my head. I've kept
the way you welcomed each guest:
candles lit at dusk on Friday evening,
sweet fruit and chilled ginger ale. *Never
hate anyone* you said, but couldn't hold to.
And if there was little love to spare
we had crisp sheets, clean underwear.

Reclamation

I've never had it before—
a place to rip up the floorboards,

disappear the interior wall
through to the stairwell below.

How naked the house seems—
exposed beams and dark cool air—

cracked, vulnerable, and, still
breathing. Irresistible

this allure, to look behind-
the-scenes to phlegm green

carpet and mouse leavings.
What is it that I'm seeking

behind this ex-closet door?
A memory vault of what

my parents might have built
if not for fear of bursting

pipes, falling trees, their children?
Each year the litany began:

gardening, fires, flood—
aren't we put on this earth to love?

Tomorrow, my carpenter
will come bringing with him

bird's-eye maple and golden fir.
He'll create a frame, build-in

a bookcase for this empty space,
this theater that's been dressed

and redressed for some fifty years.
This home moving forward—

along with the inhabitants—
to its next demolition or desire.

Emailing the Dead

July: in the fuchsia hour
far after midnight;

it happens here

our letters appearing
in the middle of mid-life

in the syphilitic
hum of the laptop

in the black pixelated lakes
spooling their cache, calibrated

through a language not my own;

forgotten scatterings
of *crème fraiche* and *en suite*

abandoned eighteen years ago
come and go again

and in the slow, download

your irreverent eyes glitter
gold-rimmed

off the slope of your animal nose.

And again I'm behind
a battered white door

the dictionary hovering
speechless like a cat

mid-air before I miss
your head, your heart, our other lives

falling forward to this summer night

where the web
site completes itself.

And we go on—
begin this talking to our dead.

You miss-type *I live with my wife
and your four children*

And what if I were a Parisian man's wife?

Your four children
our four children?

Tonight we believe we're safe—
perhaps, not.

Archive these lovely ruins
of another time

I'm still sending—

a memory that won't set
itself to sleep.

Invitation to Mr. W.

Before the birds find their breakfast, before the clack of wooden
clogs advises me of my neighbor striding to her coop,
another woman turning on the sprinklers with a swooshhhhhh.

Before I'm awake enough to call and question you again, before you
navigate with enigmatic answers and dead ends,
                    please come flying—

Over the Willamette that wends itself into town in a V,
over the Masonic cemetery replete with streetlights, verses,
                 dear, please come flying—

In this summer of my 40th year, in this season of blackberries,
cherries, and inexplicably sweet pears, won't you
                  just come flying—

Forget your double life, your despairing heart, and other minor
irrelevancies. Come with your old blue van, come with your kayak
                  but do come flying—

Over the Cascade mountains, over Allan Brothers, and Black Sun,
we'll rise above the university and be back in time for tea, so get ready
                  to come flying—

Come with me to Fall Creek, to the place where the islands part,
where we scaled rock and scree to find who we might have been
                  flying—

Come with your intense, your insistent gaze, come with silver
hair, and your body lithe, inspiring. The time is right, the landing
                 clear, come now!
Leave caution and computers and your excuses in the wind. Today,
                 before we're gone
                 please come flying—

In the Beginning

You call and offer me
June strawberries
with organic cream;
drive over with two
dishes balanced between
your knees.

You negotiate bridges,
freeways, traffic circles
then appear
undeterred by my front door.

Tilikum, Totem, Tristar—

From these blue glass bowls
we lift this moment
to our lips,
deftly fix the berries
on our tongues;

we taste what is feral,
what will keep, reshaping it
later in our sleep.

The Men You Don't Get to Sleep With

Are always the men that you want;
the ones who hide something

in their long-fingered hands
and won't let you touch it or tap it;

who refuse your good offerings
of dark chocolate and flan;

the men who come quoting
Keats, who winter in Cannes,

who summit Rainier
without ropes or brains.

These fleeting men; fantasies
we hold for years past their time,

one lone kiss from a cabinetmaker,
all night laughter with a Bosnian

jailer, the amaranth flavor
of a passionate painter. No,

that's not it, it's not what you think.
Not needing that dick but the act

of his tongue licking crumbs,
soft breath in your ear as he offers,

This is actually fun.
Caleb, Dan, the photographer man;

the ones with crushed hearts
and the ones who had none.

Damn these men, remembered
unnaturally long; did their bodies

shelter something lacquered and spun,
something even today, you wish that

you'd won? But what if sexual
climax was reached with the barista,

the sculptor, the sheik? What then?
Then what would we do?

The riddle undressed, the pleasure
no more than ho-hum.

Better to keep imagining this:
an allusive rhyme, enhanced and revised

on mountain paths, window seats,
private jets, the men that you don't get

you do get: set in pen and ink,
fantasy and less grief

they can unceasingly please.

Did You Hear, The Israelis Have Outlawed Watermelons

Prior to the formation of the Palestinian Authority in 1994, displaying the national flag was illegal. However, its colors appeared everywhere in the cut watermelons that vendors sold by the side of the road.

Picture a woman at work in a flag factory
remnants of red, green, and black fabric

unfurl as islands, torn heartlands at her feet.
Picture a Palestinian woman: stitching up the palm

of an open hand, the inside of a small boy's
chewing-gum cheek, as the tanks roll forward

into staid positions, flattened bodies
flare as heartscapes, lost islands,

an archipelago at our feet. Picture an American
woman, a caterpillar, an open hand, a young man's

chewing-gum cheek as the seamstress works
extra hours, fabric the color of bodies, cut

watermelons at her nation's feet. Split seeds
fill her palms, seeds for his lemon trees.

Picture a Palestinian caught in the camera, her gaze
flares up, overwrought, ready for release

like a caterpillar. Fragments—fruits and seeds—the old
positions. A boy's small body, a father. Everyone

sees. The woman opens her hands
a chrysalis turns the other chewing-gum cheek.

Colors, fabric, she. The inside of a seed
is a heartland. Picture a woman.

Aubade

I wake first to the pleasure of watching
you sleep; study the rise and falling

away of your body, the buttery air
as it swings itself through your nostrils.

Today, I plan to map a thousand particles
spreading themselves invisibly throughout this room.

And though that's enough said, there is more—
how bamboo sways across a lavender porch

and spider webs flicker high above floorboards—
how this joins with the sight of your shoulders:

freckled, lean, half-exposed under carnelian sheets,
to enliven me, keep me attuned to what I'm needing;

to Otis and Sarajevo as they spoon, tails curved,
nestled inside our box spring; to the scent

of jasmine flower, pineapple mint, and rose petals
climbing up through the open windows.

What is this conversation that begins in
the interchange of limbs while we are sleeping,

this slow tossing and turning, the shift of cartilage
and bone keeping their own kind of conversation?

In the moment before your eyes open, before your hand
slides its way to my waist, your nose to the nape of my neck,

I'll pretend to be dreaming, to savor this morning temple—
this unspoken source in between; blessing our each simple breath.

We Talk of What You'll Do When You Return

Invite in the warlords, text message the deadly
youth of Mogadishu

tell the women handwashing linen

Koranic students chanting
under the commiphora tree

to cancel all negotiations
abandon the gift of Global Relief.

In the dream of return
coaching family rhythms

into leagues of athletic rivalry
you'll pump up each clan, and sub-clan

to *compete, compete, compete*

not over wells to poison
or uncles, cousins, children

dead in the fields
dead along open-sewered streets.

Instead you'll imagine a world—

a wave of Olympic *torchlight
relighting Somali legend

with no angst, no anxiety.
In the counting of names

which tribe will claim the most
doctors, teachers, road builders;

which family the Nobel Laureate,
the poster child Ph.D.?

In Kismayo, the young girls fill test tubes,

invest in their own depths of discovery.
The young boy draws his life

from the sweet liquid of drainpipes
rainwater cultivating

your landscape, each acre
breathing along an open coastal sea.

Sarah's Story

I watched their figures moving light as
embroidery stitches backlit against fine cloth;

mid-summer, late afternoon baked in a lapis
blue inhalation—a day fit for any God—even Him

and those good looking angels He brought in,
their bold hips swaying as they scrambled the sea—

colored hills, bright dust lifting small circles above
their ankles. My husband napped, undisturbed, snoring

louder than our camel consorting at its bit. And so
I left Abe's arms and came to see, examining

each figure closely. It was then I sensed a stirring up,
a scouring all around my limbs, then deeper, in the interior

faultlines of my body—wide awake, at ninety—
it made me laugh and the unfamiliar sound rimmed the tent

and woke my husband, who recognized them immediately.
With nothing on but a threadbare sheet he bowed

and brayed while I left to prepare the food—
remaining close enough to listen. People ask

if I knew burning light, but I will not reply. What I know
I'll not state in scripted sounds, just imagined speech

as if in conversation, passing time with women on the street.
What meal to fix for the Lord and his company?

Brown bread, some soup, mustard sauce and lamb's meat?
Nothing fancy but they would not leave hungry. Steaming plates I set

and served and brought back again three times. The appetite of God!
Enough to make a mother wring her hands—bottomless

yet full of compliment—always a word of thanks.
Raised right I thought, the kind of son I used to want myself—

or daughter, or any child at all—I had prayed
and raged and cried for. But now at ninety, I knew

my womb was useless as a leaking chamberpot,
that a child would not bless us. Abraham no longer touched me,

though he often bragged that other women looked like monkeys
compared to Sarah's beauty. But this was habit speaking,

a slight memory of an oasis misplaced long ago. I suppose
I loved him now and again, but our bodies had forgotten how

to coax and stroke and howl, decades since I knew his hips
against my back, his thighs filling each Friday with desire

incomprehensible. And then I returned from reverie to hear Him
say *Next year when I return your wife will be with child.*

How could I *not* laugh at such a declaration?
Of course I held it deep inside my body, the laughter

that builds and fills itself, soon bridging joy
to tears in rocking rhythmic shudders.

My Response to *Happy Birthday* Emailed a Decade Late

Does time explain anything but I told you so?
Bright, traitorous, lovers seem so far from us.
If we could meet again, what more would I know?

Four cats, two books, a quiet beachside road;
yet, our emails fly shaped by Saharan dust.
Does time explain anything but I told you so?

We type *forgive*, extend the branching willow
but love's less clear than signing *keep in touch.*
If we meet again, what more would you know?

It's true you left, and now claim a small chateau,
four children, a wife, a boat that you can trust.
Does time explain anything of I told you so?

Tonight I'm sending cinnamon tea, mangoes,
blood oranges and a treaty to discuss.
If we meet again, what more would I know?

If we could live inside a kaleidoscope
would glass fracture, the colors be corrupt?
Does time change anything of I told you so?
When we meet again, what more will we know?

Scriptorium

No ink from crushed oak or smarting apples,
no swan feather quills, no Ogham stone,

just a woman of the notebook with her vision
fine pen taking up residence alone.

One long and narrow window seat, three chairs,
a desk, a stove, answer most her needs,

as she answers the page with consonants, attends
the vowels open-hearted pleas.

As the night continues on, counted out
by cups of tea, might she conceive or miscarry?

In the hard light of morning will the pigments ignite,
the words intermarry—gold-leafed, extraordinary?

Until This Evening

You have succeeded remarkably well
with the blue hydrangea by the door,

the forget-me-nots and honeysuckle
watered, fed, and told *You are adored.*

You've learned to slice an Anjou pear,
fold the towels so they'll fluff up like sails,

toss the phone when restless for salt
air, teach the cats to fend for themselves.

But the tightrope of a life asks more
than odd desires—no romantic interludes

are found behind the dryer—See!
Burnt skins of lint, breasts of colored wire.

Instead, you compensate for the shape
of your elbows, and erase the line breaks

of the clouds, re-read the crosshatch
of the kelp canopy and copy out

"Arrival at Santos," the mind
like a white-crowned sparrow.

When will the world show
better sense? Which teacup holds

tomorrow? Think star anise, water lily,
Boston fern. Beyond the house

a ferry arrives each evening—a god—
in green and white traveling clothes.

At the Corner of Washington and Third

You could start your life over, sitting here
believe only in roses,

blue oleander, an orange lily.

Clean white table with rocking chair
would be enough.

Early morning, now
the self returns to the self.

One pear scone, decanter of tea—
and the world appears terribly healthy.

In the rise of river light

open palms of poplar trees
barn swallows state swallow beliefs.

No terrorist in sight.

To the right of the fish pond
the cat claims a gray stone for her own.

The hardest thing of all

would be to choose
your own life.

—La Conner, Washington

NOTES AND DEDICATIONS

"The Exile Reconsiders" is for Ubax Gardheere.

"Mohamud at the Mosque" and "We Talk About What You'll Do When You Return" are for Mohamud Esmail.

"Mr. Saturday Night" is for Khalid.

"What You Americans Should Know: Partial Stories" is for Awale Farah.

"Nisqually 6.8": On February 28, 2001 Seattle experienced a 6.8 earthquake, its first of this magnitude in fifty years. The epicenter was located in the nature reserve of Nisqually, Washington.

"The Women of Kismayo": "Two years before the country collapsed into civil war, in Kismayo, Somalia's southern coastal city, something happened that momentarily interrupted the slow march of strife over the Body Politic." — Nuruddin Farah

"A Poem for Will, Baking" is for Rabbi Will Berkovitz.

"Did You Hear, the Israelis Have Outlawed Watermelons" is dedicated to the activism and memory of Rachel Corey.

"Not a Prayer," "White Lilacs One Year Later," "My Mother Returns at Low Tide," and "To My Mother, Dead Eight Years" are in memory of my mother, Lillian Rich.

"White Lilacs One Year Later": *Loz zikh nit shpayen in der kashe* is a common Yiddish proverb meaning "Stand-up for your rights." The literal translation is "Don't let anyone spit in your cereal."

"Sand Woman" is inspired by "Where Dwelling is Kept From Dune One Scoop at a Time," which began, "Dunes cresting at 40 feet surround the villages and smaller dunes form inside village areas between mud-brick houses; villages where so-called sand women clear doorways of sand from dawn to dusk." *New York Times*, January 14, 2000.

"In Transit" is inspired by "11 Years Caged in an Airport; Now He Fears to Fly," *New York Times*, September 27, 1999 and dedicated to Marham Karimi Nasseri.

"If You Could Lick My Heart It Would Poison You" is a line from Claude Landsmann's film, "Shoah," spoken by one of the leaders of the Warsaw Uprising.

"Iska's Story" borrows the line "You can never really write what happened anyway; it's like a hole that fills constantly with water" from Chris Hedge's account of his time as a war correspondent, *War is the Force That Gives Us Meaning*.

"Invitation to Mr. W." is with grateful thanks to Elizabeth Bishop.

"Day 7: In the Beginning" is based on the news article "Civilian Deaths Are Hard to Count" by Niko Price of the Associated Press, *Seattle Post-Intelligencer*, March 26, 2003.

Special Reports was a weekly television show produced by the South African Broadcasting Company (SABC) covering events of the Truth and Reconciliation Commission as they happened throughout the country, 1996-1998. *Braiss* is the Afrikaans word for barbeque.

"Aubade," "The House After You've Gone," and "In the Beginning" are for Patrick Donlon.

"We Talk of What You'll Do When You Return "refers to the counting of the names, a Somali tradition whereby anyone can recite their family lineage at least ten generations back. It's often said no documents were lost in the civil war; they are all inside our heads.

"Until this Evening" begins with a line gratefully borrowed from Rachel Rose, "You have succeeded remarkably well."

About the Author

Susan Rich is the winner of the PEN USA Literary Award for Poetry as well as the Peace Corps Writers Poetry Award for *The Cartographer's Tongue: Poems of the World*. Her poems have appeared in journals such as *Alaska Quarterly Review, Bellingham Review, North American Review, Poetry International,* and *Witness.* She has worked as a Peace Corps Volunteer in Niger, West Africa, staff person for Amnesty International, an electoral supervisor in Bosnia, and a human rights trainer in Gaza. She taught at the University of Cape Town on a Fulbright Fellowship and now teaches at Highline Community College in the Seattle area and in the Antioch University MFA Program in Los Angeles, California. Recent awards include an Artist Trust Fellowship, the *Sojourner* Poetry Prize, and a Pushcart Prize nomination. A community advisor for Cottages at Hedgebrook, an editor at Floating Bridge Press, and a founding member of the Somali Rights Network, she makes her home in Seattle, Washington.

Author photo by Tom Collicott.